To Francis,

Enjoy reading !

↑
The author !

Once upon a time, there was a little star in the sky named Phoenix busy planning his very first trip to Earth

"God has said to me that I can be anything I want to be".

"What shall I be" he asks himself

"I want to be a slug!" he gets excited

"I want people to know how useful the Slug is for the Earth and for Humans alike"

On a cold winter day in the United Kingdom, Phoenix has chosen his destination.

People are busy celebrating Christmas and the New Year

Totally unaware that he is getting ready for his arrival just in a few weeks' time.

How time flies! The spring is here. A little baby slug is hatched quietly with his other siblings under a large rock in the garden. Phoenix will be ready to venture out when the whether becomes milder.

Slugs are soft bodied mollusks.

Slugs are really snails without the shell. Thus allowing them a broader food source with less demand for a calcium rich diet.

Slugs are quite touchy feely creatures:)

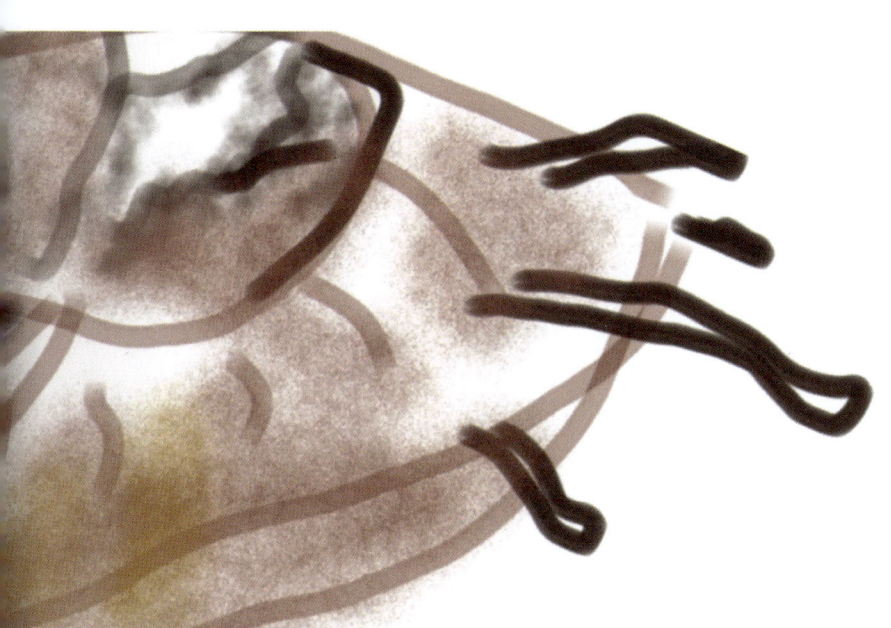

They have two upper tentacles for smell and seeing things.
The two lower ones are for taste.

Slugs can't hear so you can't call them like calling your pet cats or dogs and their eyes only see shadows

Slugs are one of the detritivores. They are like the nature's dustmen. They eat dead animals and plants. They even clear out dog fouls. The broken-down particles in their poo becomes food that feeds the soil and is ready to be used by plants.

Semi rotten leaves are good for their digestive system.

Slugs are important food for other wildlife. They attract blackbirds, thrushes, frogs and hedgehogs into your garden. Slug pellets not only kill slugs. They also kill wildlife who eat them.

It's hard to find rotten leaves during the hot summer months.
Slugs are not fussy when it comes to eating.
There are ways to protect your plants. You can also develop habitats for birds, frogs and hedgehogs.

Tall boarders, copper rings; Find slug-friendly plants; Try a slug zone with plant they love that can be doubled up as an feeding area for your bird; Or pick them up and put them in your compost bin.

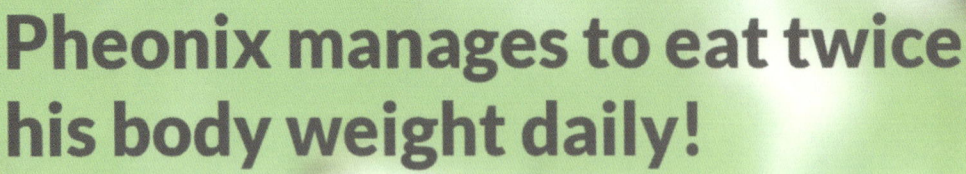

Pheonix manages to eat twice his body weight daily!

He is growing fast in size and confidence.

He has reached maturity in just 3 years

He's embarking on a journey of searching for his best friend.

Slime is particularly helpful when it comes to finding his best friend.

It can only be "the one" if the other one's slime taste right and smell right:)

Since slugs are hermaphrodites. Phoenix is about to lay some eggs.

The couple are busy finding a place under rotten logs or rocks ... Sometimes, they bury eggs under the ground. If they weren't careful, birds love to feed on slug eggs as tasty, yummy and juicy treat.

Here is a couple that I found earlier under a plant pot:))

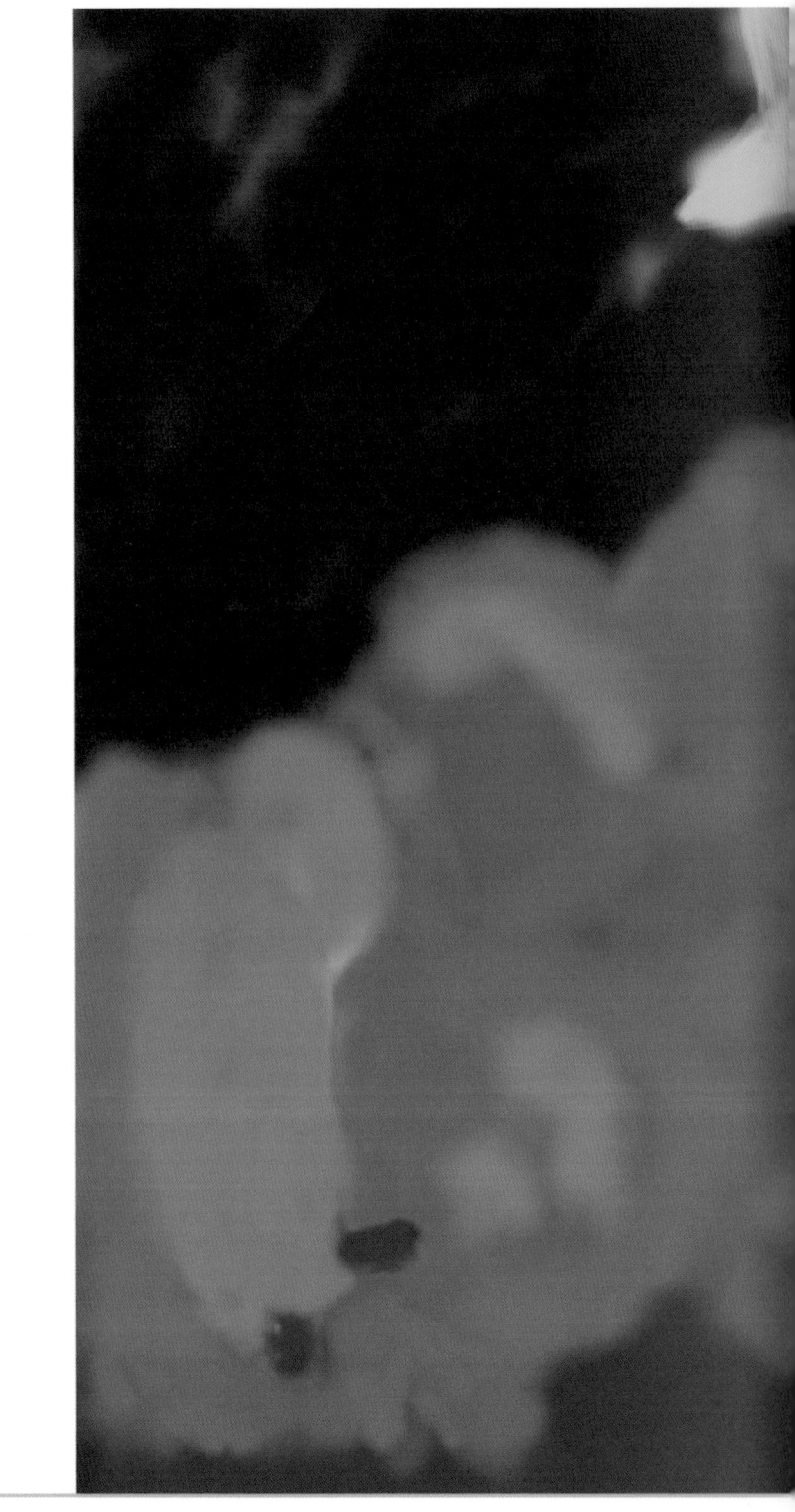

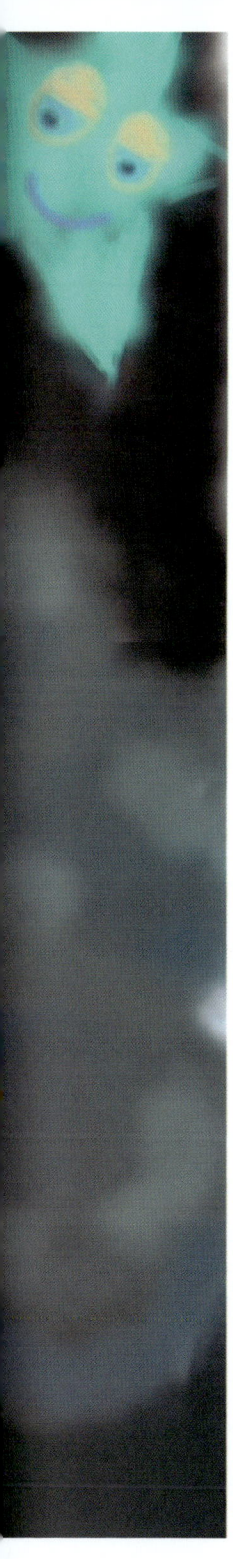

As the eggs hatch, Phoenix feels that he has completed his journey on Earth.

As he moves up into the sky, he has a smile on his face watching his babies to start a new life...

**Once upon a time, there was a little star named Phoenix ...
He was busy planning his next trip to Earth
"What shall I be?" He asks himself again ...**

Glossary

mollusks-animals without a spine with a soft body

detritivores-animals that eat dead plant or dead animal as food

digest-break down

particle-a very small bit

habitat-a natural home of an animal or plant

hemiphadite-a person or animal is both male and female

List of creatures that you want me to write about, creatures that really annoy you and you could not understand the purpose of their existence

1

2

3

Email to LilyG0221@gmail.com

Printed in Great Britain
by Amazon